TO THE ONES I LOVE

You are my INSPIRATION, GUIDES, TEACHERS, LAUGHTER,
and most of all MY LOVE.

TIPPIE – From the MOMENT, I held you in my arms,
I knew a STAR was born.

DAISY – You are WATER that brings LIFE to a tree in the DESERT.

SPIRIT – You are my TEACHER, my INSPIRATION for hope.
With YOU, anything is POSSIBLE.

NALA – My SWEETEST little girl. You are the LIGHT that SHINES in
the darkest of NIGHTS.

JACKSON – My MENTOR, CLOSEST FRIEND, and CONFIDENT.

I CHERISH every waking MOMENT with you ALL.
MOM

Author

Nyx Nightshade is a mom, entrepreneur, energy healer, and published author. Her animals and actual live events inspire her books. She is certified in Reiki, Blue Stone & Crystal Healing. She lives in Toronto, Ontario, with her horses and donkeys.

Illustrator

Andre Vitali is an internationally acclaimed illustrator / graphic designer who has lived and worked in Italy and Ireland. Andre began developing his drawing skills as a child. He Graduated in 2005 from L' Accademia Delle Belle Arti University. He lives in Monreale, Italy.

Narrator

Angela Clark is a voice artist. She has enjoyed voicing many different genres and thoroughly enjoys every aspect of voice-over. However, audiobook narration was her starting point. She always enjoyed reading, so audiobook narration was a natural progression of that passion.
She's had the privilege of working directly with several different publishers and many authors.
Angela has narrated over 150 audiobooks and over 200 hours of audio dramas.

STAY CONNECTED!

Tippie-Doo's website at www.tippie-doo.com

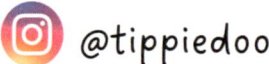 @tippiedoo    @TippieDoo   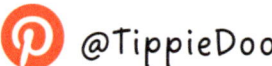 @TippieDoo

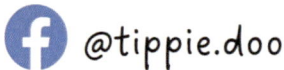 @tippie.doo   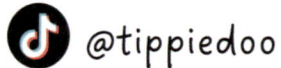 @tippiedoo    @tippie_doo

Scan the QR code to access the digital version of the book.

It is fully narrated in the children's voices by Angela Clark and illustrated by Andre Vitali.

Copyright @ 2023 by Tippie-Doo Media Corp Canada. All rights reserved.
All related titles and logos are the trademark of Tippie-Doo.
Printed in the United States of America
This book may be used for educational and entertainment purposes only.
No part in this book may be used or reproduced in whatsoever anyway or manner without written permission.

For information address, you may visit www.tippie-doo.com

www.tippie-doo.com

TIPPIE-DOO

MAMA ALWAYS HAS THE LAST LAUGH

BY NYX NIGHTSHADE

ILLUSTRATED BY ANDREA VITALI
NARRATED BY ANGELA CLARK

Hi, my name is Tippie-Doo. Well, my real name is Tippie, but my mama calls me Tippie-Doo because she says I'm a little rascal. I'm just curious because everything is always an adventure.

I have two sisters, Daisy and Nala and two brothers, Jackson and Spirit. My mama calls us all by our first name ending with "Doo" especially when we play tricks on her. It's her way of saying we are little rascals.

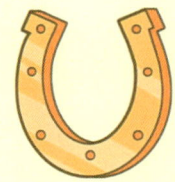

Let me tell you a story about this one time when Mama came into our playground with a bag full of treats and her lunch.

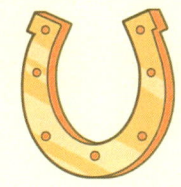

Daisy looked at me and said, "Are you thinking what I'm thinking, Tippie?"

"Are you a silly donkey? Mama's going to eat a bag of carrots in front of us for a whole week, and we are going to start dreaming about them! Oh, but those treats sure look mighty yummy, don't they, Daisy? Okay, let's do it! You run away with Mama's lunch, and while she's chasing you, I'll take the bag and hide them. Maybe by the time she catches you, she will be so tired she might even forget!"

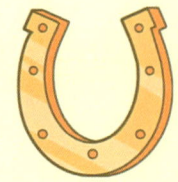

Daisy waited for Mama to put the bags down and unfold her chair. She quickly ran behind her, took her lunch, and started running across the playground.

"Daisy-Doo!" Mama shouted. "Come back here, you little rascal!"

Mama ran off to catch Daisy.

"Tippie!" Daisy yelled. "Hurry up before Mama catches me. I'm already running around like a silly donkey, and there are no carrots in this bag! I deserve more treats, or I'm telling Mama it was all your idea! She will believe me because you are the only donkey-donk who plays tricks on her."

Well, I couldn't argue. Daisy was right!

"Daisy, I got the bag! Let me go and hide it in the hay pile. She'll never think to look for it there!"

Mama finally caught Daisy. She started tugging the bag back and forth to remove the lunch bag from her mouth.

"Daisy-Doo, let go of the bag this instant!" she said. "I know you, little donkey-donk. This was not all your idea. And if you think I forgot about those treats, you little rascals, you're wrong!"

"Now, where did you hide them?"

"I didn't see any treats. Did you see any, Daisy?"

"No, I didn't see any Mama," said Daisy.

"Oh boy, you two, whatever am I going to do with you?" Mama said.

"See, Tippie, look what trouble we are in. Mama's mad!"

"Wait a minute! It was your idea to play a trick on her, not mine. I just agreed to help you! So let us hurry up and eat them before Mama finds them first!"

Mama was looking for the treats everywhere but couldn't find them.

Daisy and I ran over to the hay pile, and they were gone!

"Tippie, what happened? How could the treats disappear?" shrieked Daisy.

"Wait a minute! Tippie, whom do you think was watching us while I was busy making Mama chase me?" Daisy asked suspiciously.

"No way, it couldn't be! Are you thinking what I'm thinking, Daisy? If they did, I would tell Mama it was all their idea, so we don't get into trouble! Let's go and see if they're hiding in our bedroom," I said.

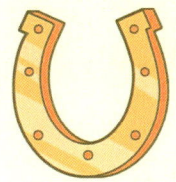

As Daisy and I ran into the bedroom, Mama followed behind us.

When she discovered Nala, Spirit, and Jackson huddled together eating the treats, she laughed out loud.

Mama forgot how angry she was and said, "This will teach you both a lesson not to play tricks on me!"

"But Mama, it was all their idea, not ours. It's not fair that they eat all the goodies, and Daisy and I don't get any!" I pouted.